10 Easy Strategies Used To Crush a Job Interview and annihilate your competitors

I0476524

By Stan Smith

Table of Contents

Foreword

The next big dream after completing your college studies is to find a good job and live a life of abundance. Most people attend college to study courses within their field of interest and develop the skills to make it through an equally competitive job market, but there are always challenges present in any job hunt in the form of the job interview. While a good number of fresh graduates are lucky enough to get the job of their dreams, some never edge any closer to theirs. The failure could be because they didn't register good grades in college or because they just don't have the experience and skills needed for gainful employment. Interviews have become quite the challenge even to those who, despite having performed exceptionally well in college, still find it hard to persuade an interviewing panel. The question is, what are effective interview strategies that will ultimately help you crush the job interview and get hired?

An interview is the questioning process or session through which you must successfully pass if you want to get hired. You may have failed multiple interviews in the past, but it is never too late to try again and again. However, it is also a fool's mistake to try the same failed approach and expect different results. This means that you must prepare more adequately for the next attempt by taking into account the tips that this book will explore in order to get hired.

Thousands of people around the globe have tried countless times to get a job, but despite having all of the right qualifications and certifications, the thought of an interview has kept many of them away from the ultimate prize. With the exception of those who prefer to start their own businesses, most people will need to go through an interview at some point in order to get a job. From the time the job vacancy is announced, the ball is set speeding towards your side of the court; this is the time to lay out the strategies that will see you seize the opportunity. The question is, how?

Your resume could have all of the aspects and hit all of the points that you think it needs, but securing the job first comes down to whether the resume capture the aspects that the *employer* thinks it needs. Does it highlight those details relating to the job you have applied for so that your prospective employer can measure your worth at a glance? A poorly written or formatted resume may not land you a job interview in the first place, but in case it does, how will you prove to your prospective employer that you are worth the price?

Further, many people have problems with expressing themselves during a job interview. This begs the question of how well you should prepare for the next interview, even if you are normally endowed with the right communication skills? You can be sure that you will fail at a job interview that is meant to hire the right candidate for a sales and marketing position or even a public relations position if you are a poor communicator. What about your appearance? How you present yourself before an interviewing panel is not only about eloquence but also has a lot to do with grooming. You must dress appropriately for the occasion so that your presentation proves your worth for the position you want to fill in the company.

While you could be endowed with all it takes to win at a job interview that has attracted many applicants, are you going to stand out as the best candidate for the job? Chances are you are set to face the stiffest competition from equally qualified applicants. Not all will make it all the way, but what about you? Devising your own strategy of facing an interviewing panel, as shall be discussed in this book, will be of great help to you, but only if you follow them to the letter. You just have to know what to do and how to do it in order to impress the employer and annihilate your competitors in your next job interview.

Introduction

Your job hunt has turned into an expedition riddled with hopelessness, and you are increasingly getting worried that you will never be employed. You have been lucky enough to secure an interview every time you have submitted an application for a job opening. However, your worry is that no job interview has ever gone in your favor. You are still unemployed. The joy that comes with getting hired is always life changing, but how many people have had this wish without it every seeing the light of day? If you are among those wishing for that big day, then you should ask yourself this question: what has always disqualified you from employment opportunities? Why is it that you have never succeeded at persuading an interviewing panel despite your good qualifications?

It is commonly agreed that always being shortlisted for a job interview but failing to annihilate your competitors by crushing the interview is very worrying. There are a number of issues that could lead to this trend. It could be that you seem disinterested in the job because you do not always have the right information relating to the job or the hiring company. Another cause could be that you are ill prepared for an interview, which could mean that you are overconfident or that you didn't rehearse enough for the big day. There are also some people who, despite being shortlisted for a job interview, have always had their hopes crushed by poor communication skills. They simply can't persuade a panel, and this comes down to the manner in which they respond to questions. Further, failing to crush a job interview could be attributed to the problem of talking too much at the expense of listening properly to the questions being asked. This is irritating and is sure to cost you the job opportunity. Further, failing to secure a job after an interview could be attributed to other weaknesses on your side, such as not being persuasive when giving answers to interview questions. A poorly presented resume and facing an interview panel as a job beggar rather than as a human resource that is eager to make a change in the hiring organization are also some factors that will easily cost you a job opportunity. Many people who have failed to secure a job did so because they suffer from all these weaknesses with little knowledge about it.

In Chapter One, we will start with one of the most crucial elements for an interviewee to keep in mind before walking into the job interview. It is all about boosting your chances by taking things a notch higher when preparing for a job interview. We will also find out in Chapter One what makes information so powerful no matter where it is applied.

Chapter 1: Information is power

If you live in this age of information, then you already know what it means to be informed on matters around you and around the world. We live in an age where information is everything, even when it comes to nailing a job interview. You must have the right details about companies, governments, and organizations waiting at your fingertips in order to succeed in a job recruitment exercise. During any job interview, you will certainly find a number of people whose desperation for employment has caused them to overlook many things that would boost their chances of getting hired. The question is, what type of information is essential for a job interview? Let's find out.

How much do you know about the company you want to work for?

The Internet has brought information about anything we might want to learn closer to us, and smartphones have made this even easier. Companies and organizations have taken advantage of the popularity and accessibility of the World Wide Web to reach out to clients and disseminate information relating to their activities much easier and faster. This is something they do through their websites. It is on these same websites that these companies place advertisements for job openings. The question is, how much time do you spend reading about companies that you aspire to work for? Also, do you take the time to surf through these companies' websites, or are you only interested in the information relating to job vacancies whenever you visit such websites?

The information age has seen companies begin to look beyond the skills and knowledge with which job applicants are endowed. They are now looking beyond the work experience you might already have. Interview questions have expanded to include information about the organization company for which you seek to work, and you can be sure that the moment you fail to answer a question relating to such information, someone who was shortlisted alongside you for the same job interview will have trashed your employment chances.

What does this mean? It means that you should never walk into an interview room with little to no knowledge about that company or organization for whom you want to work. An information-deficient brain is sure to ruin anyone's chances of getting hired, and it could happen to you if you don't prepare. The next question that you should ask yourself in this regard is, what type of information about the company is likely to inform the questions you will be asked during a job interview? This is the first step towards finding relevant information about an organization and its activities. During interviews, most companies will ask you questions relating to how you knew about them, what they do, and their vision. Other questions that you are likely to be asked include the company's latest quarterly, semi-annual, or annual financial reports, the name of the company's chief executive officer, the name of the human resource manager, and the company's objectives. These are questions worth researching so that you are always prepared with the right answers.

What does the job for which you have applied entail?

Boosting your chances of being hired is as easy as knowing the right information pertaining to the job you have applied for. You never know when a question relating specifically to the position will be asked, but if you are prepared when those questions arise, you can answer with confidence that you have crushed the interview and annihilated your competitors long before the interview even comes to an end.

Crushing a job interview and annihilating your competitors is not always just about having the required experience or the most outstanding relevant certifications or qualifications. Sometimes, being the right person for the job is about having the right information about the little things around us. Of course, it will be suicidal to face a panel of interviewers when all you know about the situation is that there was a job vacancy advertised and that you, as a desperate job seeker, threw together and submitted an application. However, even if you can somehow sail through the interview with inadequate information relating to the job, you should also know about it for your own sake. Ask yourself this question: will your employment last its full term if it is not a permanent employment opportunity?

Knowing what is expected of you at the workplace will always be a recipe for better job performance because it will see you achieve or surpass the set goals and objectives. This is why it is important to show during an interview that you know what the job involves. There are many people with great skills and expansive knowledge, but knowing too little about an organization will always minimize their employment chances during a job interview. This is because when such questions are asked, they are never able to give the right answers. Sometimes, having the right answers to these questions is as simple as going carefully through the job advertisement and gleaning the information about the job from there.

Gathering adequate information about a company as well as about the job that you have applied for has many other benefits, but above all, it guides you in preparing for a scheduled job interview. Before the day when the interview is set to take place, you should also start cultivating the necessary skills relating to the job if you don't have them already. However, it is also important to note that simply being able to recite information about a company and a job doesn't guarantee you an effortless win. This is because there are people who have waited for an invitation to a job interview, only to be told that they did not apply for the right position upon inquiry. Perhaps their cover letter indicated something else in the subject, such as a position that was not advertised among the vacancies that the company had posted online or in the local dailies. This brings us to something worth noting if having the right information remains one of the ultimate game changers when it comes to crushing a job interview. It is always important to read through the job post again and again so that by the time you put together an application, you do it correctly, precisely and with nothing but the relevant testimonials. There are also people who have applied for a job, written the best cover letter and attached the best resume they possibly could, and failed because they were missing out on critical specifications for the job.

Consequently, they never got anywhere near shortlisting because their applications were ignored. If this happened to you last time, you now know what is expected of you for the next time you apply for a job.

Chapter 2: Empowering your skills and know-how

How many times have you applied for a job and failed to secure an interview, let alone get hired? Job seekers are always in a rush to craft and send in applications. Some people even craft and submit applications in a day even though the job interview is set to be conducted in two weeks time. It might be said that the early bird will always catch the worm, but sometimes, hurrying to do something like applying for a job can ruin your chances of ever being hired. Many mistakes in the application process will have ruined your chances of having a fair stab at the job. Ask yourself this question: are you truly qualified for the job, especially with regards to being endowed with the right skills? How much do you know about the job?

As discussed in the previous chapter, a company may decide to hire a novice who only has few years of working experience instead of going for that person with at least ten years of working experience. The question is, why?

Well, you can hardly crush a job interview if, despite the many years of experience you have had doing the same job in another organization, you never bothered with empowering your skills and know-how in the field. This brings us to this question: how should you empower your knowledge and skills? While skills and knowledge alone can help you stand out from the pack of equally competitive job applicants shortlisted for an interview, what have you done as far as broadening your knowledge and sharpening your skills are concerned? Discussed below are a few ways to empower your skills and knowledge so that the next time you apply for a job, you will not just secure an interview but go on to crush it.

Problem-solving skills

Employers will always be looking for people with great attention to detail and those who have the will and desire to perform a job well. There are always some interview questions requiring at least some problem solving. This should start you thinking. How many times have you helped solve a problem – not necessarily at the workplace, but also in real life situations? Did you succeed? There is no particular job that will never require problem-solving skills, which means that you should work on your aptitude skills no mater what sort of job you intend to apply for. During an interview, questions that seek to unearth your problem solving skills will definitely edge you out of an employment opportunity if you are ill prepared. This also means that you should be thinking on your feet and making sure that you always have effective suggestions ready at your fingertips for basic problematic scenarios. Problem-solving situations also require a critical thinker who can provide real solutions. Therefore, before your next job interview, cultivate the right skills on this.

Interpersonal skills

A workplace is made up of people from different walks of life and with different attitudes. How you relate to people really matters, especially when it comes to jobs such as sales and public relations that involve interacting with other people regularly. The only way you can develop your interpersonal skills is by always being positive, even to negative people. Further, everything you do from the moment you walk into the interviewing room and exchange pleasantries with the panel to the moment you leave and beyond will influence the panel's opinion of your interpersonal skills. Remember that there will be someone awarding points for every little thing you do right, from proper greetings to a proper posture while sitting down. Make this work for you.

Make good use of vocational training sessions and conferences

Seminars, conferences, and other types of vocational training sessions have been instrumental in the lives of many employees and would-be-employees. There is always something new that you can learn from training, as long as it is relevant to your area of specialization. Also, any training that is tailored towards empowering your skills is something that you should go for.

Vocational trainings will always be an opportunity to broaden your knowledge on emerging issues and trends regarding job performance. This means that you should start looking out for seminars and conferences that would see you not only advance in your career, but also crush your next job interview. You could be the only person with such training or experience among several people shortlisted for the same job interview.

Chapter 3: The strategy that is communication

No matter how you look at it, communication forms an integral part of your life. It is unthinkable to exist without talking to each other. Interestingly, even without saying a word aloud, we will always be communicating. In the same way, job performance relies heavily on communication. Saying that communication is effective means that there is a shared meaning and understanding. There is no chance of getting hired after a job interview if you are endowed with poor communication skills. The question is how you can make sure that you stand out as a good communicator during an interview. Well, it starts with drawing the right communication strategy and working on it. Good communication is the conveyance of the right information and giving the right feedback through appropriate channels. It is the use of these channels that most interviewers will be looking for in a potential employee. Let's take a look at some of them.

Focusing on and rehearsing speaking skills

Any employer will be looking for someone who is practically perfect when it comes to words articulation but will hesitate to hire an applicant who is whispering out answers during an interview. You should make it clear that you are good speaker from the time you enter an interview room and exchange pleasantries with members of the interviewing panel. If you are unsure of how good your skills are when it comes to speaking, rehearse and have someone listen to you before walking into the interview room. Some people rehearse their speaking skills before a mirror, which is equally effective as long as you mean business.

Gaining composure

Using too many gestures to convey a message or respond to a question can be very irritating and even intimidating. In a job interview, this predicament would obviously be a bad one. Your chances of being hired will have plummeted to zero. A job interview is an official setting that requires professional but interactive communication. Make it easier to be understood by limiting your usage of gestures. Your facial expression during an interview should also show that you are composed and responsive. There is no way that you will be hired for a job after the interview if your facial expression is constantly a frown or indicates that you are not interested in the job. Develop a facial expression that is sure to create warmth in the interview room. It is also imperative that you rehearse proper posture before the interview, especially if you are not accustomed to it. Taking these into consideration will surely boost your chances of being hired.

Audibility and eye contact build confidence

If you have ever attended a job interview before, did you look down throughout the session? How often did you maintain eye contact with the interviewers? Confidence during an interview can be gauged based on many aspects, including you maintain eye contact with those asking you questions. However, the eye contact should not be so intense or extended as to come off as defiance. Keep it soft, but not to the extent that it will also portray you as shy person. If this is unimaginable, the best way to go about getting it right is through practice and rehearsal before you attend your next interview. Practice makes perfect, and rehearsing properly reflecting your confidence is a sure way to boost this undoubtedly important skill. For practice, you can have a few friends, and maybe a few strangers, ask you questions and try to respond while maintaining friendly eye contact. In fact, through proper eye contact, you can win the trust of a prospective employer and crush a job interview instantly.

Another aspect of confidence that will keep you on par with your competition during an interview session is audibility. How loud are you when responding to questions? Perhaps you have never been hired because whenever you attend a job interview, the way you respond to questions can be interpreted as shouting. However this is a curable problem. The best way solve the problem of shouting answers during a job interview is, as always, to practice, which will help you develop the right pitch and voice intonation.

Dress code as a first impression

You will similarly never be hired if you attend job interviews without paying proper attention to your dress code. An interview is not always only about being knowledgeable or having an outstanding resume supported by a dozen testimonials. How you dress is equally important and is sure to give you a competitive edge when it comes to scoring high and crushing a job interview. Dress code is a powerful non-verbal cue that interviewers will use to determine, among other things, your communication skills and attention to detail. Always be sure to confirm with your mirror, friend, or spouse that you are properly dressed for an interview before leaving the house.

Chapter 4: A substantially filled resume

Employers are always looking for smart recruits, which is something they can quickly judge by taking a look at the resumes of the job applicants. Simply defined, a resume is a brief overview of one's academic background, professional achievements, experiences, and personal interests. Whenever there is a job opening, most companies will require applicants to submit a resume alongside a cover letter prior to the interview. A resume helps an employer catch an invaluable glimpse of one's potential, and in some instances, employment decisions will be made based solely on this fundamental requirement. The use of a resume has become so ingrained in every employment culture across the world that even before a job opening comes up, everyone is in a rush to craft a perfect resume and have it delivered in good time once the opportunity presents itself. Essentially, a resume is a vital element for anything that relates to job application, and it is on this premise of its indispensability that people always strive to create a solid first impression by using resumes before meeting. This always takes place long before one faces a potential employer through a job interview. The question is, how can you crush a job interview using a resume and annihilate your competitors? Even though it precedes an interview, a well-written resume is sure to boost your chances of being hired even before an interview is conducted. Here are some tips that will help you to fine-tune your resume and stand a high chance of being hired.

What should appear on your resume, and what should not?

A resume is a form of self-marketing magic, a characteristic that many have more often than not overlooked. This has continued to limit the chances of many people when it comes to employment. Your resume should have value in it, which brings us to the issue of what you need to include in it and what should be left out.

Most people apply for jobs that meet their personal interests, experience, and academic qualifications. This means that they will always express their interest in vacancies they feel suitable enough to take on, but while many do this, a resume that is devoid of details relating to the job in question can indicate otherwise. A resume should be short and precise, a characteristic that makes it easy for a potential employer to review. Imagine a situation in which about five hundred applicants have expressed their interest in a job opening and sent in a resume. In order to compete against time, an employer will likely spend a maximum of three minutes perusing the resumes of applicants. The use of this process to see the right person get hired will always rub a number of applicants the wrong way, especially those with unnecessarily long resumes of up to, say, twenty pages. This means that to be among the best candidates for the job, your resume should only include content relevant to the job you have applied for. For example, don't include content relating to a teaching experience if you are applying for a position in sales and marketing. Also, keep in mind that there will be people who make the mistake of applying for the same job as you using the same generic resume that they use for every other job. Exploit this weakness by tailoring your resume to the job specifically.

Resume wording and formatting

The way your resume looks can either boost your chances of getting hired or ruin your hopes completely. Thousands of people around the world, while applying for jobs, have shown little to no consideration regarding using the right words and formatting styles when compiling their resumes. If, for example, you have working experience in a technical field such as process engineering and you want to apply for a job with little to no technical aspects, then the trick is to tone down your technical wording while perfecting your formatting.

While it is suicidal to send the same old resume to tens of prospective employers, using the same format can also spell doom. This is especially true if the job opening to which you are applying requires a simple-to-follow structure and easy-to-understand language. It would be an unthinkably bad idea for an Information Technology specialist applying for a sales job to use the same IT language in the application. If this becomes the case, you can bet on ruined chances. What does your resume look like? What is the readability level of your resume? What is your choice of words? These are questions that should make you consider aspects of word document formatting, such as alignment, spacing, font type, font size, and typefaces. It is important that you use a consistent typeface, font size, and spacing, for these are the aspects that would most enhance the readability of your resume. No employer has the patience or the time to strain to read a resume that is packed with words and inconsistent in formatting. Most companies will post guidelines on the formatting styles they need to see in applications; if they do, be sure to properly follow the instructions in the job post. The aspect of language register is also pivotal if all you need out of an interview is to get an edge over your competitors and get hired. Here, you ought to take into serious consideration the level of language you use, especially with regard to terminologies. Every field is unique in terms of language, which is something you should understand before sitting down to craft a resume. Use medical language if you are applying for a job in medicine, but don't use the same language if you later apply for an IT job opening.

Resume appeal and presentation

How your resume looks is its 'appeal', and how it is delivered is 'presentation'. Are you the kind of a person who does not follow the formatting rules for word documents but still expects to be considered for a job position because you believe that you have what it takes? If you fall into this category, then you are mistaken. The same way airhostesses dress the part, so should you dress the part when it comes to crafting an appealing resume.

You will only have yourself to blame if a potential employer throws your resume into a bin because it looks awful, but remember that this is something you can easily avoid. It takes patience to craft a well-formatted resume that is sure to help you crush a job interview. This should be crowned by the way the resume is presented. How do you deliver your resume? While most companies will give guidelines for application presentation, in most cases it is left to common sense. Make sure you deliver your resume, which is usually accompanied by other documents like testimonials and cover letter, in a neat and clean envelope or folder. This is both professional and clearly communicates who you are. However, it should be noted that an eye-catching resume that is lacking in substance will still not take you anywhere near shortlisting.

Chapter 5: The interview: facing the panel the right way

For most job seekers, the most defining moment of the process is facing an interview panel. This is the time to either show your worth and crush the interview or let your competitors annihilate you. Most people experience an adrenaline rush during a job interview, which clearly manifests through restlessness, sweating, not responding to the right questions, and avoidance of eye contact. Before we delve into these, let's take a look at some sample questions that might be asked of someone seeking to be recruited. Practice answering the question for yourself based on the job you wish to apply for, taking special care to pay attention to the guidelines after every question. Also, in this sample live interview, we only take into consideration the questions that most employers, if not all, are likely to ask you – you are in no way guaranteed to get all of these questions or *only* these questions.

Question One

Interviewer: Tell me about yourself.

Interviewee: (How are you supposed to respond?) However this may sound, this question does not want to know about your biographical data as captured in your resume or information relating to your age, where you come from, your religion, or your marital status. Rather, it seeks to find out your professional experience, achievements, and skills. In most interviews, this is will the first question asked, and unless you did some pre-planning and research, you will be disadvantaged and may not qualify for the position you seek to be recruited into.

Question Two

Interviewer: How much do you know about this company?

Interviewee: (Guideline for responding) This is another obvious but deceptively tricky question that companies or organizations will often post to interviewees early in the interview as a means of reducing the number of applicants successfully shortlisted for an interview to a more manageable number.

This question takes us back to Chapter One, where we delved into preparing for a job interview under the chapter heading: Information is Power. Companies today seek people who are reliably informed about the world around them, and this is a question that can make or break you during a job interview. To answer this question satisfactorily, doing prior research is important. This you can do by taking a look at the company's website and reading extensively about its services, products, management team, and structure, as well as other factors like its vision, goals, and objectives. Talking about the life history of the company won't win you a job.

Question Three

Interviewer: Why are you interested in working for this company/with us?

Interviewee: (Tips for responding) This is a question that leaves many in a state of confusion, but as long as you did your research about the company exhaustively, it becomes an easy obstacle. The best way to answer this question is by talking about the company's inspiring progress, success in being an equal-opportunity employer, reputation in the face of competition, and the many opportunities for growth it offers to employees. Don't go into issues like the salary scales, as this may just ruin your employment chances.

Question Four

Interviewer: Tell us about the benefits you are expecting.

Interviewee: (How to reply) This is another question that features in most interviews and always requires utmost honesty in answering because failure could mean that you are hired at a salary with which you are dissatisfied. Ostensibly, this question seeks your salary scale proposal, but it is always wise to ask the interviewer first about how much they offer for such a position. Remember that you should always negotiate for better terms of employment unless the company has a sufficient reason for paying less than what you have asked for.

The best way you can go about this is by doing prior researching on the salary that the company pays its employees. You can do this by approaching some its employees directly.

Question Five

Interviewer: Tell us why we should hire you.

Interviewee: This is another question that is quite tricky, especially for those who do not know that it seeks to find out how much you have achieved in the line of your profession both for your former employer/current employer and for yourself. It will be a clear indication of whether you are worth hiring or someone else takes the position. The best way to edge you way out of this question satisfactorily is by talking about the accomplishments in your resume. Be honest because someone will be looking at the resume you had previously submitted while you are responding to this question.

Question Six

Interviewer: In your working life, have you ever been fired or sacked?

Interviewer: Just like it was the case when responding to the question about the benefits you expect from the company, this is another question that requires the utmost honesty. If you have ever lost a job through being fired, be honest and give a clear explanation for the reasons that led to it. With the information age upon us, the credibility of any answer you give can be verified and any lies will only work against you.

Question Seven

Interviewer: Is there anything in particular that you liked about your previous job?

Interviewer: (Tips for responding) Employers are always wary of those who seek to get an opportunity at any cost, even if means badmouthing the previous companies they worked for. As a result, this is another question that seeks complete honesty when it comes to responding. If you loved the challenges in your previous job, talk about them and explain how they made you better.

Talk about the opportunities for growth offered to employees. Never be afraid to talk about negativities, but be fair and objective. This is not the time to talk about poor or better payment, and such answers should be avoided at all costs.

A good response to this question calls for proper pre-planning before the interview in case it features among the questions that will be asked.

Question Eight

Interviewer: Have you ever been assigned a leadership role in your current or previous job?

Interviewee: As much as this could and should be captured in your resume, echo what the resume says in more detail. If you had been assigned to a supervisory role over a taskforce or a group, explain the responsibilities that the position required in detail.

These are among the many obvious questions that you should always be prepared to answer because they are highly likely to appear in any job interview. The better you prepare for them, the better your performance will be at the job interview and the better your odds of annihilating your competitors. Having gone through the interview, let's take a look at some other tips and prerequisites that would help you crush a job interview instantly.

Confidence markets your potential

Employers who are seriously seeking to recruit productive people for job openings will be consciously categorical when it comes to confidence. Teamwork is the new trend in most organizations when it comes to accomplishing tasks, and it requires confidence in handling challenging tasks and relating to others. The question is, how do you boost your confidence before the interview? Practice will always make perfect, but before you set forth on a job interview, rehearse your presentation of your confidence to ensure that it is on par with what the job expects of you. The opposite of confidence is low self-esteem, and you can be sure this will not land you a job anytime soon.

Low self-esteem always has negative effects not just on how you relate with others, but also on your communication skills. As you enter an interview room, be sure to exchange pleasantries zealously and confidently. This can be done easily through firm grip during a handshake, and with that you will have scored highly in this part.

Sitting confidently with your hands placed on the table is another milestone during a job interview. An upright posture during an interview is an indication of confidence, but you should avoid fidgeting or any other annoying unconscious behaviors. Do not let your confidence spill over into overconfidence. It will cost you a golden opportunity because interviewers will feel like you are looking down upon them. Remember, dressing is part of the process of boosting your confidence for an interview, so dress well for the occasion.

Responding to questions

During an interview, the only way to annihilate your less-prepared competitors is by giving the right responses to the questions you are asked. This takes us back to the sample interview discussed above. Always stay positive, relevant, precise, and upbeat. Do not avoid questions because if you do, crushing a job interview will become a nightmare for the rest of your life. For questions that demand an explanation, be relevant and explicit, and for questions that demand one-word answers, ensure that your response is appropriately short.

Eye contact as a window of reliability and confidence

This varies depending on the society's culture. In America, for example, eye contact during communication is a show of truth, confidence, and trustworthiness. Maintaining eye contact with interviewers is a crucial component of portraying confidence, and it also indicates honesty as far as the answers you will be giving are concerned. Here, there is no option, and practice makes perfect.

Every minute counts during an interview, so make good use of time

During an interview session for a job that has attracted tens of applicants, time is a valuable resource. In this regard, crushing a job interview will be related to pertinent issues like time management.

Employers get irritated by interviewees who waste a lot of time thinking about the right answers to give, as well as by those who do unnecessary things like fidgeting and pondering over their copies of applications and testimonials. Make every minute count, and you could just crush a job interview.

Show the interviewing panel that you are a resource, not a liability

Employers are never interested in poor time managers, and applicants who will turn out to be a liability to the organization rather than a productive human resource will equally ruin their own employment chances. From the onset of an interview, you can show your resourcefulness to a prospective employer in a number of ways. In fact, the best way to be sure of crushing a job interview and annihilating your competitors is not by creating an *impression* of productivity and resourcefulness, but by showing you really do have the skills and the know-how.

The question is, how do you go about this? There are simple attributes that many ignore but that if developed and presented, will cast one into the limelight as a productive and resourceful person. One such attribute is time management skills. The ability to save time can be depicted by the precision with which you will have crafted your resume and the quick, precise, and reliable responses you will be giving during a job interview (refer to the sample interview previously discussed). Another way through which your resourcefulness will be manifested during an interview is through punctuality.

Punctuality during a job interview is important and because companies are not only competing against time, but also against competitors. Therefore, showing them that you are a good time manager will be an added advantage. Not everyone will be punctual for an interview, but for an interview where you are the only shortlisted candidate, be sure to arrive minutes before the interviewing panel.

Chapter 6: Presentation and Grooming

Did you know that an interviewer has the discretion of making up his or her mind on a potential employee from as early as the time you set foot into the room and exchange pleasantries through a handshake? To ladies, taking substantial amount of time in front of the mirror might be habitual, but what about men? Presentation refers to appearance, and in this context, how you prepare for an interview is paramount. On the other hand, grooming is a broader aspect of presentation because it takes a look into bits and bytes of enhancing your physical appearance. Essentially, good grooming is a recipe for proper and appealing presentation.

How many times have you turned up for an interview and felt that something was not right with your dress code, shoes, or hairstyle? How did you come to notice it? Well, the way you look in terms of body grooming can either attract people to you or repel them. This is equally true in the case of a job interview. From the time you enter an interview room, you can notice something about your grooming based on how the members of the interviewing panel react. Do they smile and nod appreciatively or look down? Find out next time you attend a job interview, but to this end you know what to do.

Many people believe that getting hired for a job they have applied for is based on being endowed with the requisite skills and knowledge. However, when such people fail to make it through an interview despite their enormous skills, they start to look for scapegoats and even start saying the interviewer or employer was this and that. But did you know that you could have ruined your own chances by not appearing for the interview in the right attire or dress code?

Like it or not, how you look during a job interview is equally as important as your qualifications. An interview schedule is not the time to showcase your taste for fashion and trendy dressing styles. It is a time to look courteous and sharply dressed.

In this chapter, we take a look at how presentation and grooming are part and parcel of the whole process that will see you crush a job interview and annihilate your competitors.

Good grooming is an important first impression

Appearing for an interview is always a stage in the whole process that could change your life forever. That is to say, how you dress will either elicit in your prospective employer an interest in hiring you or simply be a turn off. When dressing for an interview, wearing high-end official attire is not negotiable. You must dress the part. For a lady, dressing scantily would be distracting, and the interview will definitely not favor you. It is important to dress for the occasion because how you dress will be the basis upon which the interviewer will form a first but lasting impression of you. This is something easy and should therefore provide you with the opportunity to crush a job interview and consequently annihilate your competitors. Remember that a picture is often said to be worth a thousand words, and there is no way you can change this conventional view of appearance and imagery. You have to look professionally good because a job interview is not a fashion show.

Grooming as a sign of care

For jobs like sales promotion and marketing, the first impression you give will be the one expected of you should you be hired for the job. When companies post job openings on the web or in the local dailies, they are always specific about the attributes they are looking out for in potential recruits. An example is attention to detail. How you dress for a job interview will make this attribute examinable.

People who dress well for a job interview create an impression of attentiveness to detail, while those who could care less about their appearances come off as careless and are never hired. By being well groomed in hairstyles for men, hairdressing for women, and dress code, you come off as someone who not only cares for personal hygiene but is also keen on details.

Good grooming elevates your self-esteem

Self-esteem is a necessary attribute that any employer will be looking for in an interviewee. Through good grooming through appropriate dress code and general appearance, you will be casting an image of confidence, which is a desirable quality any employers look out for in a potential recruit. Employers want to hire people who can present themselves well, and they can judge this from the way you have dressed for an interview. So if you have been taking this lightly, make a good show of it during your next interview, and you could just be hired instantly.

Fundamental tips on grooming for an interview

Here, you would want to ask and answer the question of what you are supposed to do with regards to grooming before an interview. This is as simple as ensuring that your fingernails are well cut and that your hair is neatly cut if you are a gentleman or appropriately styled if you are a lady. An important part of presentation is that you should not chew gum during an interview because this will be irritating and disruptive. Furthermore, have your portfolio folder or briefcase well cleaned. You should also ensure that your shoes and teeth are properly cleaned and that your pockets are emptied so that there is nothing protruding from your clothes.

The clothes that you put on for a job interview, apart from being official attire, should be well ironed to remove any creases that would paint you as careless. Regarding usage of grooming items like body lotions, perfumes, bathing soaps, and deodorants, always ensure you have used them sparingly.

A lot of perfume would not create a friendly atmosphere for an interview because there could be one or two members of the interviewing panel who are allergic to strong scents.

In summary, grooming and presentation are core necessities that arouse in a prospective employer the right or wrong perception of an interviewee. This therefore calls upon you to make efforts to look good, presentable, and positive before you appear for your next interview.

Chapter 7: Listening and Speaking

Listening and speaking together form an important and indispensable part of communication. Both listening and speaking are skills that anyone seeking to become a good communicator must cultivate. While you could have not gained the best listening and speaking skills back at school, they are skills you can always practice to perfection. In this chapter, we take a look at how listening and speaking are equally important to anyone who wants to crush a job interview. Because employers will always be looking for people who can express themselves through effective communication, the skills of listening and speaking become important inert abilities that will either show or not show at all during a job interview. The truth is that employers will gauge your speaking and listening skills during the interview so that they can be sure of hiring the right person.

To this end, you should ask yourself this question: how will the interviewer know you are not just a good speaker but also a good listener or vice-versa?

Do you listen more or speak more?

While talking and hearing are passive processes, listening and speaking are active processes that at the end of a communication situation will yield meaningful ends such as shared meaning, shared understanding, and the giving of appropriate feedback. This means that crushing a job interview requires good listening. In fact, during a job interview, it is advised that you speak less than you listen because this is the only way you are able to understand and give the right responses to questions being asked. In the event that you start to speak more than you should during an interview, you will most likely lose points in communication skills.

For jobs that involve a lot of customer relations such as sales and marketing, the only way to deliver productivity at the end of the day is by being a good listener. This is because as much as you will be required to respond to inquiries about services and products, you will be spending more time listening to clients' needs and complaints. Therefore, next time you attend a job interview, make sure that this is seriously taken into consideration if you want to annihilate your competitors.

What is the rate of your speech?

Sometimes, the things that make a person fail a job interview turn out to be simple preventable mistakes. For example, speaking so fast that you can't control your breath could cost you a job opportunity. For one, the interviewer or members of the interviewing panel will have a hard time trying to figure out what you are saying. Speaking too fast is mostly caused by nervousness. The adrenaline rush becomes so much that you start to shiver and sweat during a job interview. The question is, how are you supposed to adapt so that the next time you face an interviewing panel, you are at ease with yourself and able to give clear answers? The best way to counter this problem is through practice. Human beings are generally said to utter about 150 words per minute, so going beyond this will translate to a faster speaking rate that will undoubtedly inconvenience your listeners. The best way to tone down your speaking rate is to read words written on a piece of paper. For this practice, you can write 200 words on a piece of paper, read them out loud on a timer, and notice if you finish in a minute or less. If you do, you need to work on a more moderate speaking rate. This is a speaking skill that, if well cultivated, will definitely help you crush your next job interview.

Avoid interruptions

Words and ideas can sometimes overwhelm you during a job interview and cause you to interrupt the interviewers. This will only cause massive problems. Interruption of speakers has always been interpreted as rudeness, and it might just see you sent out of an interview room. Most people interrupt speakers with little knowledge of doing it. This means that those who interrupt don't always know that they are doing it until they are told to exercise some level of courtesy and speaking manners. If this is habitual and seems to happen to you every time you attend a job interview, it is advised that you go back to the drawing board and start practicing good speaking skills. However, sometimes it happens to people for whom it is not a habit. In such a case, the best thing to do is apologize to the person interviewing you so that the session doesn't result in an argument or a bad impression. Remember, you are attending the job interview to showcase your capability, not to give a lecture. Do it in the most orderly manner possible and with courtesy because this will boost your chances of crushing the job interview.

How good listening and speaking skills will help you give the right feedback

Let's begin this with a question. Have you ever attended an interview, only to realize afterwards that you gave wrong answers to some questions? This happens to everyone and to someone every day. Sadly enough, most people never take time thereafter to find out what the cause of such a blunder could have been. Speaking and listening skills are important elements in any communication situation, and as long as you are not fully engaged in the process of an interview, there are high chances that you will misunderstand the questions and consequently give wrong, irrelevant, or unclear answers. This just shows you how poor speaking and listening skills can cost you a job interview that you might have otherwise crushed.

Why do employers hire good speakers and good listeners?

When it comes to good speaking and listening skills and qualifying for a job, there is no bargain. As previously pointed out in this chapter, good listening skills are essential for certain jobs like sales and marketing that lay special emphasis on communication skills. Sales promotion is a job centered on speaking, and unless you are endowed with effective speaking skills, you can hardly make it in a job interview tailored towards recruiting a sales person.

Further, another reason why you should display good listening as well as speaking skills during a job interview is that apart from the skills helping you annihilate your competitors, prospective employers always view a good speaker and a good listener an efficient problem solver and critical thinker. Critical thinking and problem solving arguably have a strong connection with good speaking and listening skills. Numerous studies have proved this. Therefore, before your next interview, sharpen your listening and speaking skills beforehand if you want to increase your chances of getting hired.

Chapter 8: Responding to Questions

An interview is a two-way communication process. There is always a time when an interviewee is given a chance to ask questions, but the bulk of the process is made up of questions asked by an interviewer and responses given by an interviewee. The channel of communication is, in most cases, verbal for live interviews and non-verbal for interviews that involve filling and submission of questionnaires.

During an interview, an interviewer and an interviewee communicate through the appropriate channels, including verbal and non-verbal communication. The communication is definitively face-to-face, and this should be a springboard for any interviewee when it comes to learning how to respond correctly to the questions that will be asked. In Chapter Five, we discussed ways to face the panel and looked at a sample interview while providing tips that will help you answer interview questions effectively.

However, responding well to the questions is only part of the whole process. After this chapter, you will have learned not only to respond to questions correctly but also how you are supposed to do it.

Responding to the right questions

Answering interview questions can be a daunting task, especially if you have not gone through Chapter Five of this book, but again, here comes another interesting twist regarding responding to the right questions. During an interview, how will you know that you are responding to the right questions? The first step towards knowing that you are giving answers to the right questions during an interview goes back to what was discussed in the previous chapter on listening and speaking.

The only time you should speak is when giving responses to questions, which means that you will be spending more time listening to the interviewer asking questions. However, in the event that you do not properly understand the questions, you have the discretion of asking the interviewer to repeat or explain the question before you proceed with giving answers. There are also some circumstances that can make you give wrong answers, such as hearing problems or the interview taking place in noisy environment. However, in most cases, an interviewer will take into consideration possible limitations that can interfere with the interview by providing hearing aid if need be and ensuring that the session is taking place in an environment that is free from noise or visual distractions. If these are taken care of, then you will have no excuse for giving wrong answers to right questions.

Feedback channel

Another critical component for responding to interview questions is the channel of communication. As mentioned before, it is always important to know and understand beforehand the channel of communication that will be used during the interview. While most job interviews are always face-to-face verbal communication, others could take the form of writing as a channel of giving feedback or even use both. Therefore, responding to the right questions would only be achievable if you know beforehand the channel of communication that will be used and as a result are able to adequately prepare for the big day. You will definitely gain a competitive edge over other applicants shortlisted for the same interview if you are already informed on the channel of communication that will be predominantly used, and you can be sure of crushing the job interview and annihilating your competitors. The feedback channel is therefore an important consideration that you should take note of before facing an interview panel to respond to questions.

The place of non-verbal cues when responding to interview questions

As noted earlier, some interview sessions involve more than one channel of communication because there is time for live face-to-face communication and time for filing questionnaires. However, when it comes to non-verbal questions, a proper self-appraisal should be made during the whole session. This should be based on the question, are you using a lot of non-verbal cues during an interview? One bit about non-verbal cues that can ruin your job hunt is that some are interpreted as abusive. This means that you should know ahead of time what your culture recommends as the right signs. The first handshake you exchange with your interviewer is one such non-verbal cue that can land you a job instantly because it would have communicated a lot about your self-esteem.

However, while it is advisable to use appropriate non-verbal cues such as facial expressions and bodily movements sparingly during a job interview, overusing these cues or using the wrong ones could cost you a golden employment opportunity. For example, shrugging during an interview could be considered abusive or an indication that you are not interested in the job. Similarly, smiling too much could indicate a lack of seriousness or ridicule. It is also against interview rules to fidget, play with your fingers, bite your lips, or make unnecessary body movements. Apart from the non-verbal cues, clarity of voice when responding to interview questions will also help you to score big. It will not only depict your readiness for the interview but also reflect your communication expertise. If you have always had problems with voice projection when responding to interview questions, practice makes perfect. The earlier you start, the better.

It is important to note that the moment you learn how to use the right channels and use non-verbal cues sparingly, any job interview will be smooth sailing.

It is also worth noting that non-verbal cues are sometimes used alongside verbal cues to reinforce a meaning or an answer. For example, when a question demands a "yes" as an answer, the conventional way of reinforcing this is by nodding upwards. However, nodding sideways when you mean to say "yes" will be confusing. While some of these skills are simple and obvious, there are people who have failed countless interviews because they either lack the skills or are simply taking things for granted.

Chapter 9: Making the interview interactive

Making the interview session more lively and interactive depends on the interviewee, but how are you supposed to achieve this in order to enhance your chances of crushing the interview? Making a job interview interactive is part of the efforts that can ultimately get you hired, but only if you do it the right way. It will definitely be a game changer and ensure that you will have annihilated your competitors by crushing the job interview.

Job interviews are not wars to be fought. Rather, they are communication situations through which one seeks to display his or her professional prowess and academic achievements for employment considerations or job placements. Most people go into a job interview with the notion that it is a lifetime opportunity that must just be grabbed, and so they do it with fear. However, to those who have always faced a job interview with a smile, it has always been a smooth ride that has seen them get hired. What does this mean?

Going into a job interview while wearing a frown or an emotionless face will not land you anywhere near being employed, but why? This brings us to the main issue of our discussion: how are you supposed to make a job interview interactive?

Shape your communication skills

Communication is pivotal when it comes to job interviews because however it is conducted, it is will be a process of shared meanings and understandings and the giving of proper feedback. The way you display your communication skills is sure to make an interview interactive and ultimately win you your dream job. Communication is a skill acquired through practice, and while everyone can be subjected to the same training session, how one applies the learned skills during a job interview makes all the difference. You are most likely to get hired if you leave the panel in stitches of laughter at the end of the interview. Imagine a situation where you have attended a job interview, and at the end of the session, the panel thanks you for putting a smile on their faces. Your hopes of filling the vacant position will have definitely been raised higher than you could have anticipated. While it is important to look serious during an interview session, a reasonable sense of humor makes you outstanding, and the prospective employer will instantly start viewing you as someone intelligent and able to communicate well with coworkers. If this happens to you during a job interview where competitive sales promotion recruits are being sought, then expect good news in return. Expect the much-awaited call saying, "You are hired."

Most employers believe that to be able to communicate a message effectively, one must arouse some sort of reaction in the recipient. That reaction could be in form of laughter, a frown, a smile, or another type of non-verbal expression. However, when you are speaking and no one seems to be reacting to what you are saying, then it will be quite discouraging. It is an indication that you are probably saying nothing that interest them and that you have to work out something in a limited time to protect your chances.

Asking questions is a recipe for an interactive interview session

Smart people always have a way of showing their intelligence anywhere and anytime. When it comes to a job interview, getting hired does not come on a silver platter; it is decided through a competitive process that will see a number of shortlisted applicants left out. This elicits the question, does asking questions enhance your chances of being hired?

The plain truth is that it really does. However, asking irrelevant questions will make you ruin even the limited chances you might have. During an interview, there is a time for every party to be engaged.

This takes us back to the previous chapter where we discussed issues to do with when to respond to questions and when to ask for clarification should you fail to properly understand. In this regard, compare two different interviewees who are simultaneously asked questions throughout the interview but do not both ask questions at the end of the session. There is a high chance that the one who asked questions will have crushed the interview and as a result annihilated the quiet interviewee. What about the type of questions that are you supposed to ask in order to make the interview interactive?

In most cases, interviewees are allowed ask questions at the end of the interview session. However, the questions you are supposed to ask should show your enthusiasm for the position. Examples include: to whom will I be responsible for reporting should I get hired? Is there a job description for this position? When will you be making a decision for this position? Asking these and similar questions will increase your chances of being considered for the position.

Be energetic, dynamic and knowledgeable

Employers hire resourceful applicants to fill vacant positions in their companies. How are you supposed to make a killing out of this knowledge? During an interview, you should come out as a resourceful and productive applicant through asking questions and responding clearly and honestly to every question from the interviewers. If you do this, there is no doubt that you will have crushed the job interview.

However, there is something more to asking questions and explaining your answers. When answering questions or giving explanations during a job interview, it is imperative that you do so with zeal, energy, and dynamism.

There is a big difference between someone who responds to questions with a lack of enthusiasm and someone who does so with massive interest. In this regard, you should do a bit of explanation using non-verbal cues to reinforce the meaning of what you say without becoming distracting.

Chapter 10: You are a human resource, not a job beggar

In the previous chapter, we looked at factors that can enable you make a job interview interactive or enjoyable. In this chapter, we will take a dive into something even more important if your goal for a job interview is a successful hire. Everyone who attends a job interview must have been shortlisted for it, and this sets the stage for a competition where the best candidate will annihilate the others. You believe that you have what it takes to perform the job should you get hired, so this chapter will explore the issue of human resourcefulness.

Among those who attend a job interview, there are those who are desperate for the position, and there are others who believe that their qualifications and performance at the job interview will get them hired. This makes it possible to distinguish between a job beggar and a human resource. The question is, what will make you stand out as a human resource rather than a job beggar? How will you show the interviewing panel that you are worth being hired for the position advertised?

First and foremost, as discussed in Chapter One, your level of knowledge will either be powerful enough to get you hired or weak enough to see you left out. It is important that whenever you attend a job interview, you do so in full understanding of what the company expects of you. This will differentiate between you and another person who attends the job interview without any knowledge relating to the job advertised and the company's activities. Stand out from the pack as a resourceful person endowed with the right knowledge and skills, ready to take on the job if a chance is offered.

Another distinguishing characteristic of a human resource is communication skills. It is hard to exist without communication, and this translates to job performance. The best communicator will always crush a job interview as long as communication is one of the skills being tested. Being endowed with the right communication skills is arguably resourcefulness that any employer will be looking for. Because you now know, practice to perfect your communication skills.

Nevertheless, a resume is a powerful communication tool, especially when it comes to job application and job placements. At the very least, it can quickly portray you as either qualified or unqualified. There are many people who have never gone beyond applying for a job. However, for those who edge closer to being hired, part of the success is always credited to a good resume.

As discussed earlier, make your resume stand out because it will earn you a good reputation beforehand. Notably, you should never fill a resume with false information because this will automatically get you disqualified. It simply means that you ought to make it look worthy by ensuring that what you pen down in a resume is relevant to the job you are applying for. Even if your competition is submitting voluminous resumes, long, descriptive resumes do not give them a gateway to an interview. It is also important to take note of the fact that shortcuts will only hurt your image in the long run if you are hired and you cannot perform the job as required.

There are ostensibly many ways of displaying your resourcefulness and prowess aside from those discussed here. Even personal presentation can show your potential employer that you are the right person for the job. However, do not let pride cause your fall by overdoing or oversimplifying things. Moderation is advisable.

Conclusion

Having read through every step of preparing to crush a job interview and annihilate your competitors, what remains are the practical bits and bytes of it. Are you going to keep employing the same old tricks that have seen you hunt for a job for years on end, or are you going to implement this useful e-book to help you land a job in your next interview? Your guess is as good as mine, but a step-by-step implementation of this e-book is the ultimate path to crushing a job interview. It might not take a day, but with consistent practice, it will ultimately prove its worth.